State of Siege
[Users Manual]

Copyright © Gefen Publishing House LTD
Jerusalem 2003 / 5763

This book is a joint publication of:
Gefen Publishing House LTD and
Israel@heart
www.israelatheart.com

Concept and Design: Doron Goldenberg

Translated from Hebrew by Fred Skolnik

1 3 5 7 9 8 6 4 2

Gefen Publishing House
POB 36004, Jerusalem 91360, Israel
972-2-538-0247
orders@gefenpublishing.com

Gefen Books
12 New Street Hewlett,
NY 11557, USA
516-295-2805
www.israelbooks.com

Printed in Israel
Send for our free catalogue

ISBN 965-229-310-5 [alk. paper]

Library of Congress Cataloging-in
-Publication Data
Goldenberg, doron, 1973-
State of sige: [Users Manual]
/ by Doron Goldenberg
p. cm
1. Arab-Israeli conflict--1993- --Pictorial works.
2. Terrorism--Israel--Pictorial works.
I.Titel.
DS119.76.G62 2003 · 956.05'3--dc21
CIP NO: 2003040885

Grave sites waiting for the dead

Existence
Reality, Experience, Being

urvival; Self-Preservation.

Dream
Imagination, Vision, Hope, Yearning, Ideal.

1967

War's End

The war of the Sons of Light against those who wished to rain down darkness upon us had ended.

Four enemy armies had been defeated and destroyed; a glorious chapter in the history of the Israel Defense Forces had come to its end.

All the Land of Israel was in our hands. Jenin, Nablus, Tulkarm, Kalkilya, Ramallah, Jericho, Hebron, Bethlehem and Gaza had been conquered. All the West Bank ours. All of Sinai ours. The Temple Mount ours. All of Jerusalem ours. The Cave of the Patriarchs and Rachel's Tomb also in the hands of the children of Abraham, Isaac and Jacob. We had returned to the holiest of our holy places, never to be parted from them again.

The Israel Defense Forces were stronger than ever, glorying in victory, sure of their ability to preserve the peace just as they had won the war.

The days of mourning and bereavement had ended; we held out a hand of peace to our Arab neighbors, with greater earnestness than ever before.

["] The Israel Defense Forces in Their Finest Hour, Victory Album, Six-Day War, Misaviv L'Olam Publishing House, 1967.

HALT! You are about to enter an area under the jurisdiction of the Palestinian Authority. Entry prohibited!

IMPORTANT NOTE
BY THE AUTHOR

This book was conceived at a time when the State of Israel is facing relentless Palestinian terror.

Following the collapse of the Peace Process and the beginning of the second "intifada," the Israeli public was filled with fear and many had lost hope in the prospect of a peaceful future.

This book is my attempt to portray the mood in Israel during this period. Through my book, I hope to awaken Israelis from the passivity that I believe has engulfed many in our society. The situation is very complex. While I know where I place most of the blame, I am also aware of our share of mistakes. To the reader, the picture I have portrayed may appear gloomy, but let me remind you that life here in Israel continues in a relatively normal way, despite the tension. Israelis go to work, school, the beach, the shops, and they go about their business, just like people in any other country. Most importantly, the citizens of Israel live in this country of their own choice. Israelis continue to live here with the belief and knowledge that this is their homeland and their rightful place in the world.

Doron Goldenberg,
Tel Aviv, January 2003

We are hopeful that if Americans are exposed to the Israeli perspective, they will identify with Israel's struggle.
In October 2002, Israel at Heart brought 48 Israeli university students to the United States as 'ambassadors for Israel' to speak on college campuses, and also in synagogues, churches, and high schools, both Jewish and non-Jewish. The speakers did not focus on politics but rather on day to day life in Israel. Israel at Heart actively encourages tourism and study trips to Israel. We also stress the importance of studying the Middle East conflict in order to defend and support Israel against verbal attacks.

ISRAEL AT HEART

Israel at Heart is a non-profit independent organization that promotes a better understanding of Israel and her people. We believe that Israel is unfairly portrayed in the media, and her significance as the only free democratic society in the Middle East is not being conveyed to the public.

INTRODUCTION
BY JOEY LOW

Television audiences might be forgiven for believing that the nightly news presents the whole picture of the Israeli-Palestinian conflict. The broadcasts are by now familiar. A blown out Israeli bus, charred and smoking. Survivors sitting by the roadside, shocked and bleeding. Israeli tanks rolling into dusty Arab villages. The words "cycle of violence," "terror" and "retaliation".

But how does it feel to be walking down a street, knowing that at any moment, the next explosion might engulf you and those around you? What is it like to go to work on a bus, hoping it will remain intact for the journey?

While I was visiting Israel last July, a friend suggested I drop in at Bezalel, a leading art school in Jerusalem. The seniors were presenting their thesis projects. Of the sixty graduating students, seven had chosen to focus on the situation in Israel. Here was an opportunity to catch a glimpse of the ways in which young, talented, artistic Israelis viewed their lives and their country.

My friend arranged a viewing and an interview with the seven students. Each conveyed a very different, but equally moving and sensitive interpretation of the situation, reflecting the diverse spectrum of reactions and opinions that is a hallmark of Israeli society.
Doron Goldenberg was the last of the students I saw that day. In his powerful work, he captured a sense of the impact of terror that can't be reproduced on television. Also, he created a visual tool that conveys a mood – a sensation – that can't be communicated via a newsreader. Doron and I spent many hours together. He explained to me the meaning and significance of each of the 200 pages in his book. I was convinced of the importance of translating this book into English, so that Americans and others could share, in some way, a very talented Israeli artist's impressions of an intensely difficult period in Israel's history.
I hope that readers will gain a better understanding of the daily struggles Israelis face and consequently will be inspired to assist Israel during this time of crisis. May we all pray for a better future, and peace in the days ahead.

Joey Low,
Founder of Israel at Heart

01 State of the Nation

State: the totality of conditions in a given reality

Dear Citizens

1. Israel is in a state of emergency.
The economic, political and security situation is subject to many crises. In this time of cruel and bloody struggle, the boundaries between the battle front and the home front become blurred. The whole nation is the army, the whole country at times a battle front. Every one of us, at any moment and in any place, must hold him or herself responsible for the defense of the State of Israel.

2. The situation that has been forced upon us is fraught with peril and demands awareness and preparedness to ensure personal safety. It is your duty as citizens of the State of Israel to be on the alert, to keep your eyes open to what is happening around you, and to guide your family with wisdom.

There is no room for panic, only to act intelligently.

3. Please continue to exhibit presence of mind, to do what is expected of you efficiently and unstintingly, to place all your inner resources at the disposal of the nation.

All of us together, and first and foremost the army, will defeat our enemies.

4. In case of suspicion or any incident, dial 100* and report it to the police.

5. With best wishes for peace and security for the nation.

[*] 100 is the Israel's equivalent of 911 in the U.S.

In thos

The peace process with the Pales

And thus suicide bombers swept into the arm

there

Many said, at first haltingly, then

in train stations, in cafes, in shopping malls, in discotheques, in cater

great

does not have anyone to talk to

in the West Bank and Gaza Strip snipers waited and ai

for the

is the sky falling in but

them. In the main streets of the big cities car bombs detona

Isr

e days

nians, in all its phases, collapsed.

th people going about their business on buses,

was

raight out, that the State of Israel

ls, in pedestrian malls, in crowded crosswalks. In roadside ambushes

danger

the other side and that not only

sts of fire at passengers in passing cars and killed

State of

earth too is trembling.

n a distance burst in the air sowing death and destruction.

el.

["] Orli Castel-Blum, Human Parts

State of Israel

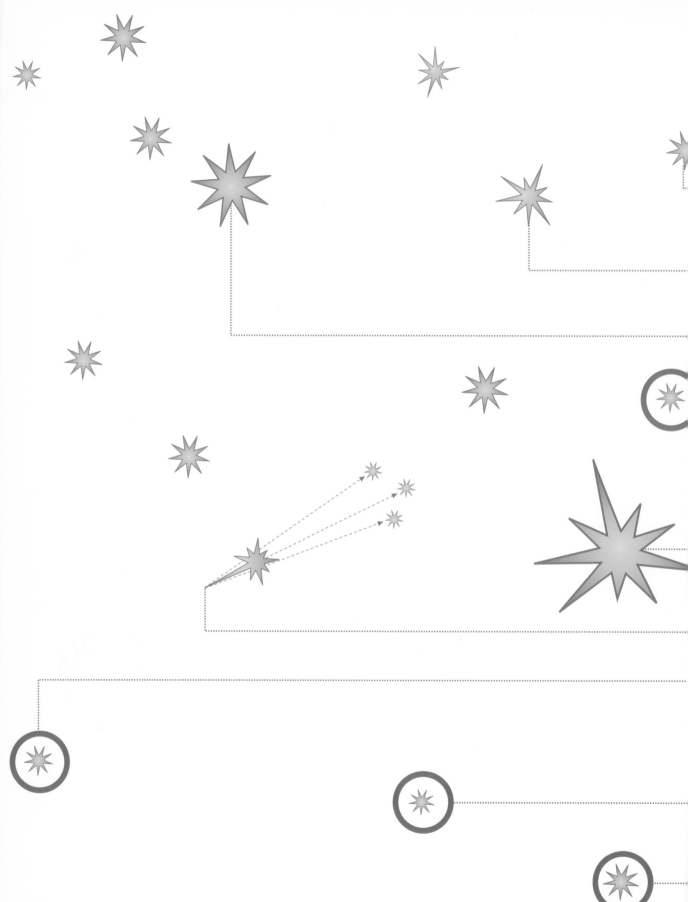

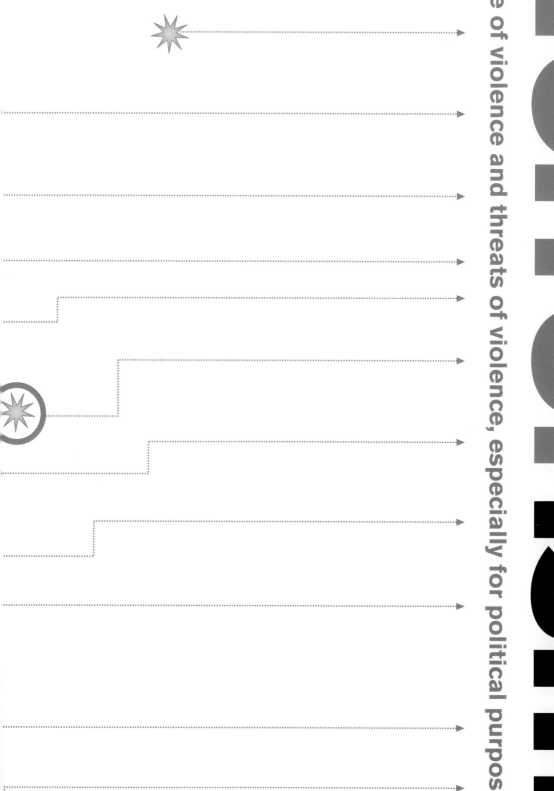

Terrorism

Use of violence and threats of violence, especially for political purposes

Street

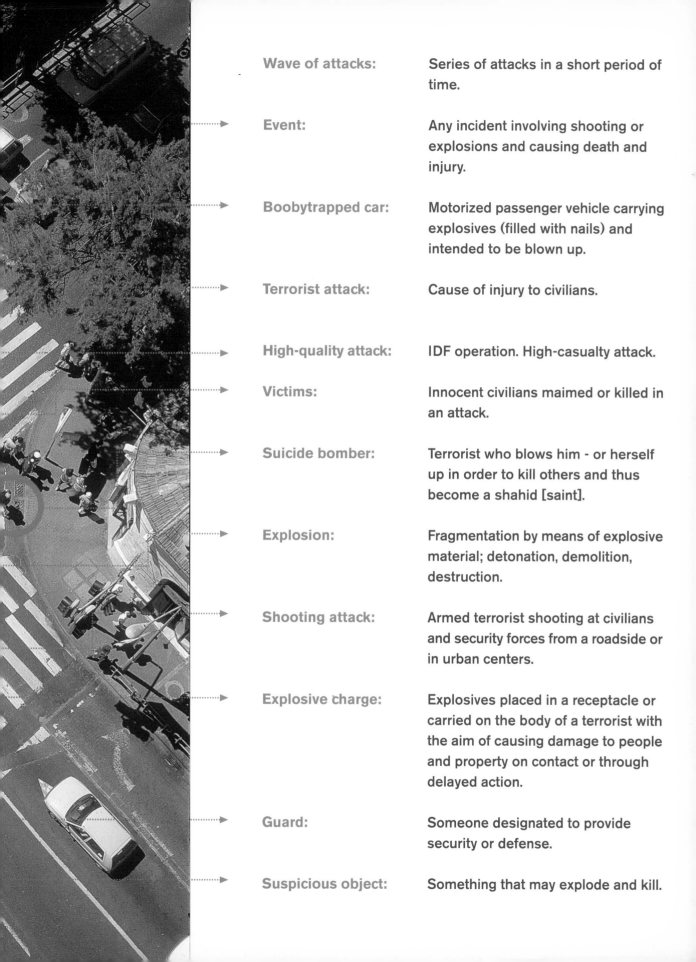

Wave of attacks: Series of attacks in a short period of time.

Event: Any incident involving shooting or explosions and causing death and injury.

Boobytrapped car: Motorized passenger vehicle carrying explosives (filled with nails) and intended to be blown up.

Terrorist attack: Cause of injury to civilians.

High-quality attack: IDF operation. High-casualty attack.

Victims: Innocent civilians maimed or killed in an attack.

Suicide bomber: Terrorist who blows him - or herself up in order to kill others and thus become a shahid [saint].

Explosion: Fragmentation by means of explosive material; detonation, demolition, destruction.

Shooting attack: Armed terrorist shooting at civilians and security forces from a roadside or in urban centers.

Explosive charge: Explosives placed in a receptacle or carried on the body of a terrorist with the aim of causing damage to people and property on contact or through delayed action.

Guard: Someone designated to provide security or defense.

Suspicious object: Something that may explode and kill.

City:

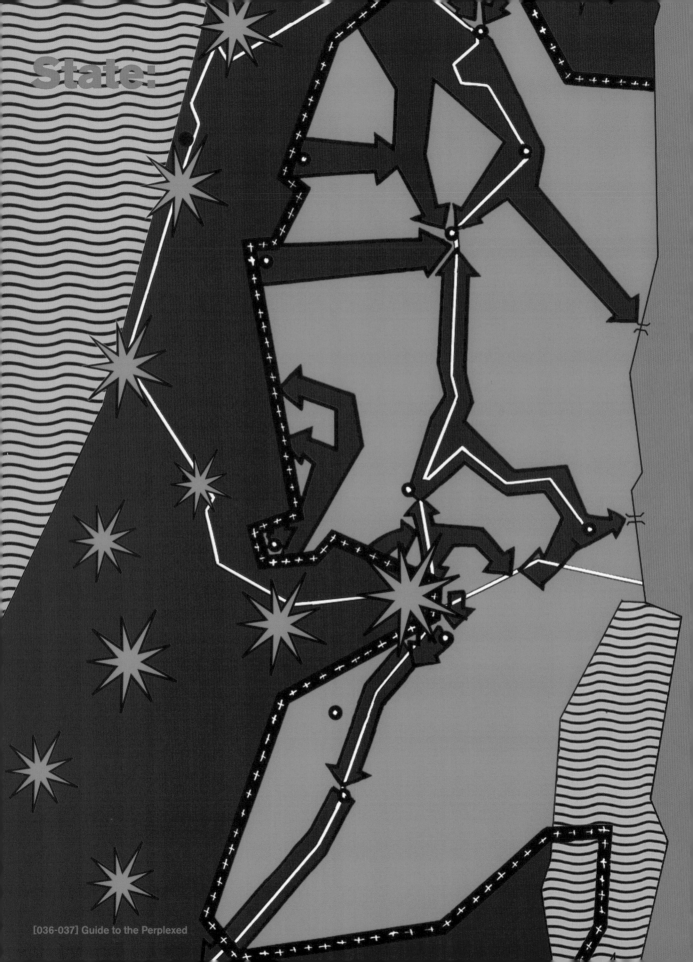

War of the Blues and the Reds

Chain of Events;

Development, occurrence of consecutive events developing one from another.

Response;

Reply by word or deed to the act of another; result of stimulation.

Revenge;

Punishment deriving from inner need to hurt a person who has injured or insulted; payment in kind; eye for an eye.

Restraint;

Self-control, forbearance; abstention from revenge.

After 100 years of fighting and attempts to live together in peace, two colors found themselves engaged in a war unlike any that had preceded it.

[1] The Sneak Attack Two Reds sneak up on the roadblock and open fire. The five blues manning the roadblock are killed.

[2] The Kill One of the Reds runs to the barracks while the second covers him. One Blue is killed, a second wounded.

The response of the Blues is not slow in coming.

[3] The Raid The Blues arrive at a building undetected.

[4] The Break-In Blowing out the door gets them inside.

[5] The Hit Armed with silencers, the Blues fire at the Reds, wiping them out and collecting abundant terrorist armaments.

The Reds hasten to revenge.

[6] The Ambush The explosive charge is ignited and the Reds open fire.

[7] The Clash The Blues return fire.

[8] The Explosion

The Blue tank that is brought in goes over a Red explosive charge and blows up, with three Blue dead and one wounded.

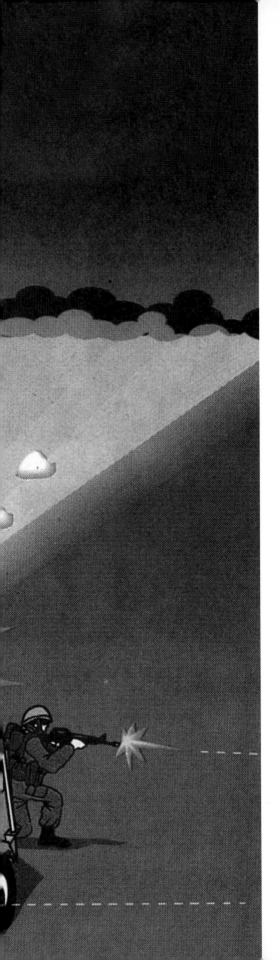

Given the magnitude of the incident the Blues cannot fail to respond.

[9] The Trap The Blues capture a dangerous Red on their wanted list.

[10] The Demolition A Blue bulldozer destroys the house of the wanted Red.

[11] The Accident A wall of the demolished house falls down and kills the commanding officer of the Blues.

Despite the threats and harsh reprisals of the Blues, the Reds continue to exact revenge with even greater violence.

[15] The Car Bomb

[12] The Gunfire

[18] The Assault

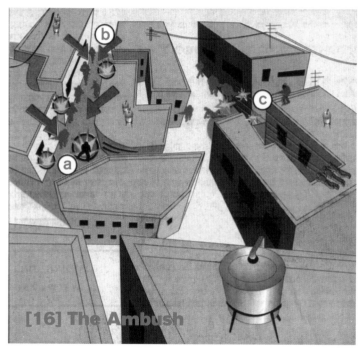

[16] The Ambush

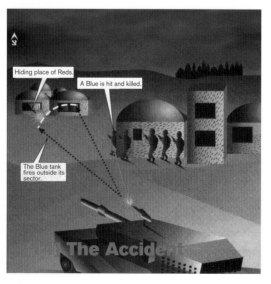

Hiding place of Reds.

A Blue is hit and killed.

The Blue tank fires outside its sector.

The Accident

[17] Explosion 2

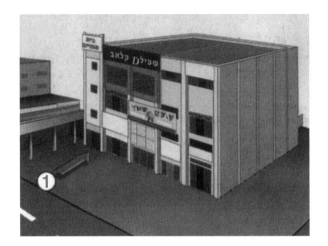

1

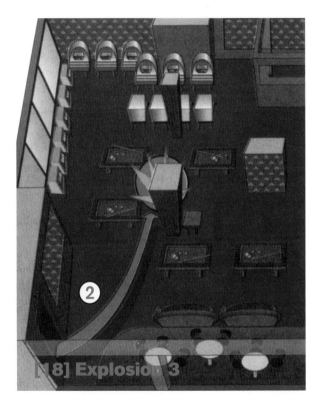

2

[18] Explosion 3

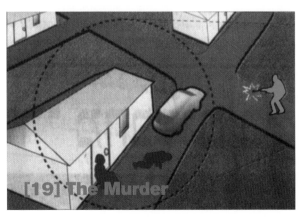

[19] The Murder

[20a] The Kill

[20b]

[20c]

[20d]

[20e]

[20f]

[21a] The Catastrophe

[21b]

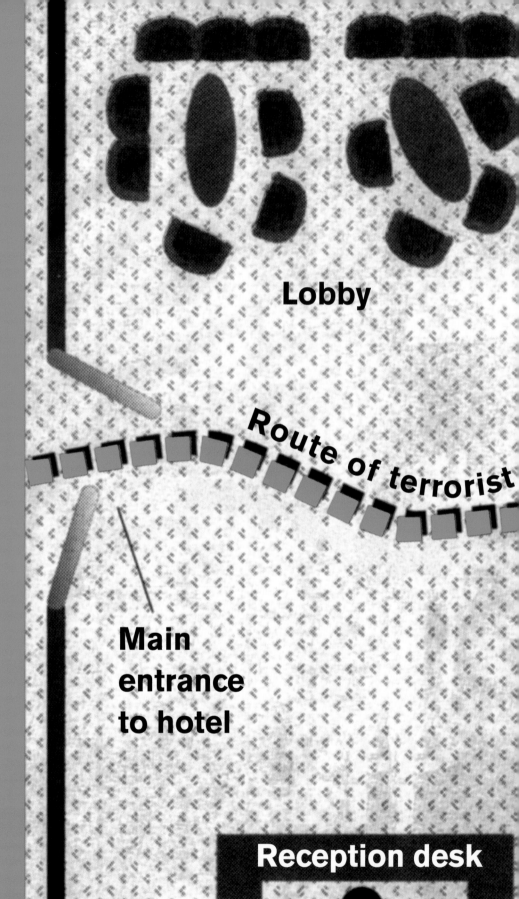

Lobby

Route of terrorist

Main
entrance
to hotel

Reception desk

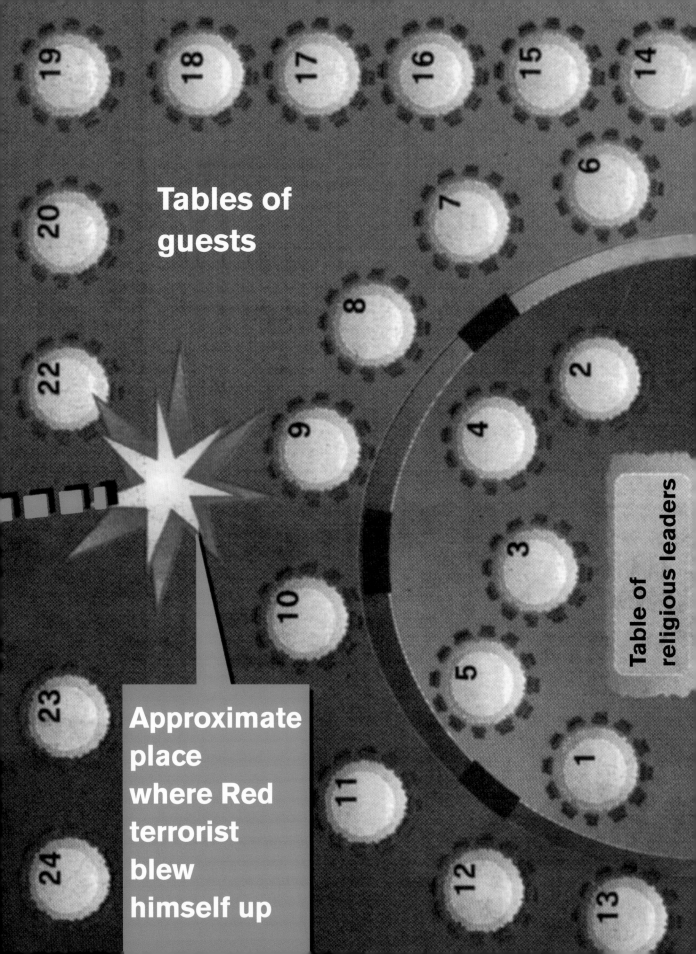

After a long period of restraint, the Blues decide to retaliate and settle scores with the Reds and their leaders.

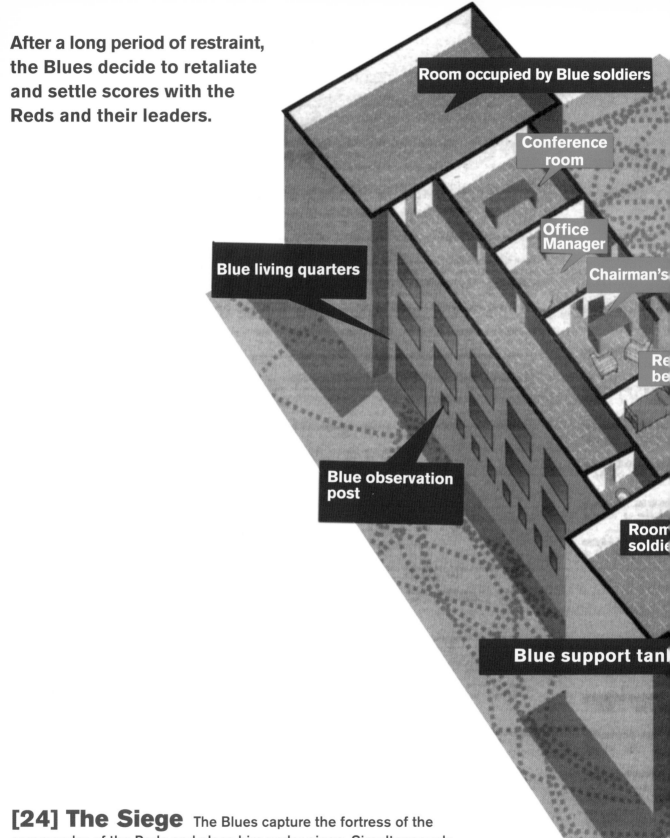

[24] The Siege The Blues capture the fortress of the commander of the Reds and place him under siege. Simultaneously they capture all the cities of the Reds and in this manner hope to eliminate Red terror.

03 Democracy

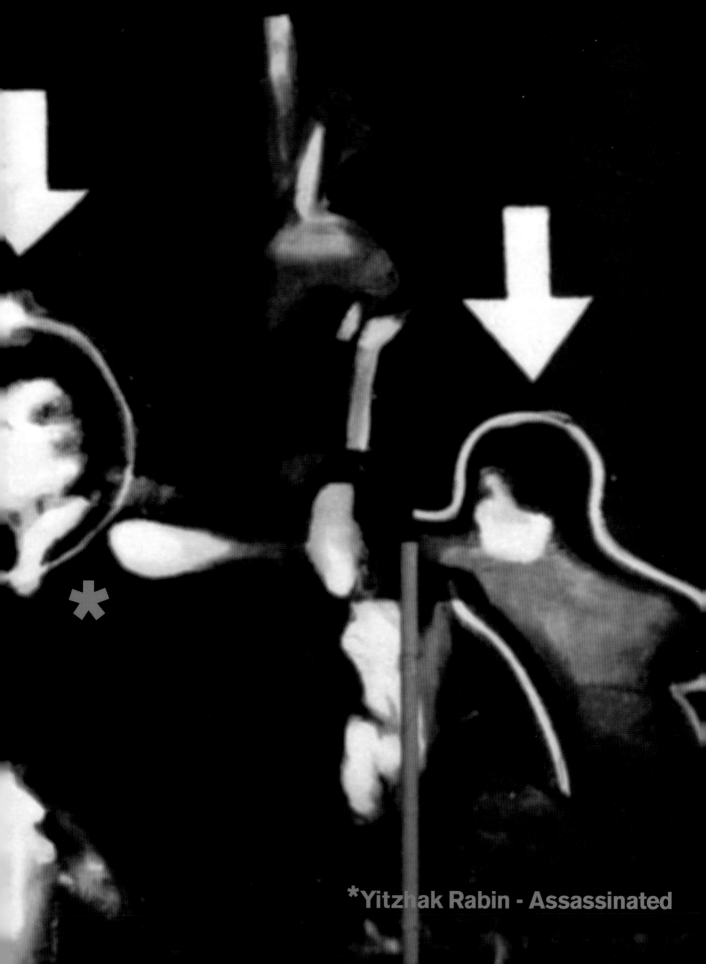

*Yitzhak Rabin - Assassinated

*Shimon Peres - Beaten

ביבי נתניהו, העם צמא להנהגת

העם רוצה

העם מחכה

בחסות מסעדת האווזים בנמל ת"א   שמעון דהו

רק נתניהו הביא ביטחון.
רק נתניהו יביא שלום אמיתי.
נתניהו.
מנהיג חזק לעתיד ישראל

 אהוד ברק
למען עתיד ילדינו

 אהוד ברק
למען עתיד ילדינו

 ברק
דינו

 אהוד ברק
למען עתיד ילדינו

 אהוד ברק
למען עתיד ילדינו

אהוד ברק
למען עתיד ילדינו

*Ehud Barak - Unseated

*Yasser Arafat - Chairman of Palestinian Authority

The Israeli Prime Minister's Chamber

פיגוע ברא

קרן נויבך

מבט הרוג אחד וכ-20 פצועי
התאבדות במדרחוב במר

VE ON THE PHONE

JERROLD
KESSEL

CNN

NG NEWS
ST 16 KILLED,
URED
N RAIN & FOG NEAR TUNIS, TUNISIA.

CNN

S&P 500 ▼ 3.18

החדשות 2

בראשון לצ

ה נוימן

מד"א: כעשרים נפגעים פונו
לבתי החולים

גור צלליכין

Newscasting

ד הלר

רח' השילד

רח' הכרמל

תידחוב תחנה
מרכזית

בפיצוץ במועדון בראשל"צ

LIVE
SHINGTON

SUICIDE BOMB

החדשות 2

משה נוסבאום

אזור תעשייה חדש

Y NEWS
LASH

BREAKING NEWS
REPORTS: 15 PEOPLE DEAD IN
EXPLOSION NEAR TEL AVIV

געים באולם שמחות
שייה החדש בראשל"צ

החדשו 2

אזור התעשייה
החדש

מתי כ

INSIGH

BREAKING NEWS
SUICIDE BOMBING NEAR TEL AVIV
KILLS AT LEAST 10, WOUNDS OTHERS

פיגוע במועדון סנוקר בראשל"צ
יש הרוגים, כ-40 פצועים פונו לביה

TRANS-ATLANTIC ROW OVER STEEL.

החדשו 2

אודי כ

החדשות

גל גבאי

אזור תעשייה
חדש

ל"צ

פיגוע במדרחוב בראשון לציון
עשרות נפצעים

געים באזור התעשייה
ל"צ

1. The Place

2. First Pictures

תמונות ראשונות ממקום הפיגוע, בראשל"צ

3. Security Forces

פיגוע התאבדות במועדון סנוקר בראשל

4. Rescue Workers

פיגוע התאבדות במועדון סנוקר בראשל"צ

שידור ישיר

5. Condition of the Injured

אלי נינין

6

נפצע בפיגוע

6. Mr. Minister

7. The False Condemnation

Yasser Arafat

8. Taking Credit

אבל לנו יש
מטרה אחת,

Sheikh Yassin, Head of the
Hamas terror organiztion

הלילה

9. The Response

רוני דניאל

Explaining the
military action

10. The Names of the Dead

Shalom. In the attack. First news report. About ... dead. About ... injured. We'll go to the body of the suicide bomber. What can you tell us. According to police estimates. A spokesman for Magen David Adom. Here's the report of. The names of. Unbearable. More than ever before. Witnesses to the explosion. Apparently we have here. For those joining us now. All of a sudden I heard. I saw. To this point the following has been released for publication. We'll get back to you. Good evening, Mr.

Minister. I think we have to. As you know, I. Yes, but what should be done. Live from the hospital. The condition of the injured. Escalation. Good evening, MP. As someone who. I don't recommend. I disagree. At this difficult time. What's the answer. We'll get back to you. We'll be back after this. How many, how many? In the last analysis. How can one grasp. There's no choice, we have to go on. The funeral will take place. We can say the incident is over. An additional warning. **The weather.**

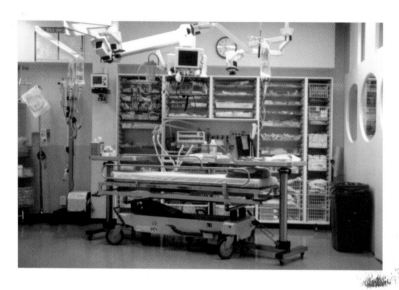

"Everything is ready for the next attack" [Channel 2 News]

05 All of a Sudden

**All of
a sudden
I heard:**

[↑] A police specialist is disarming explosives from a terrorist's body　　　　[↑] Neutralizing a bomb

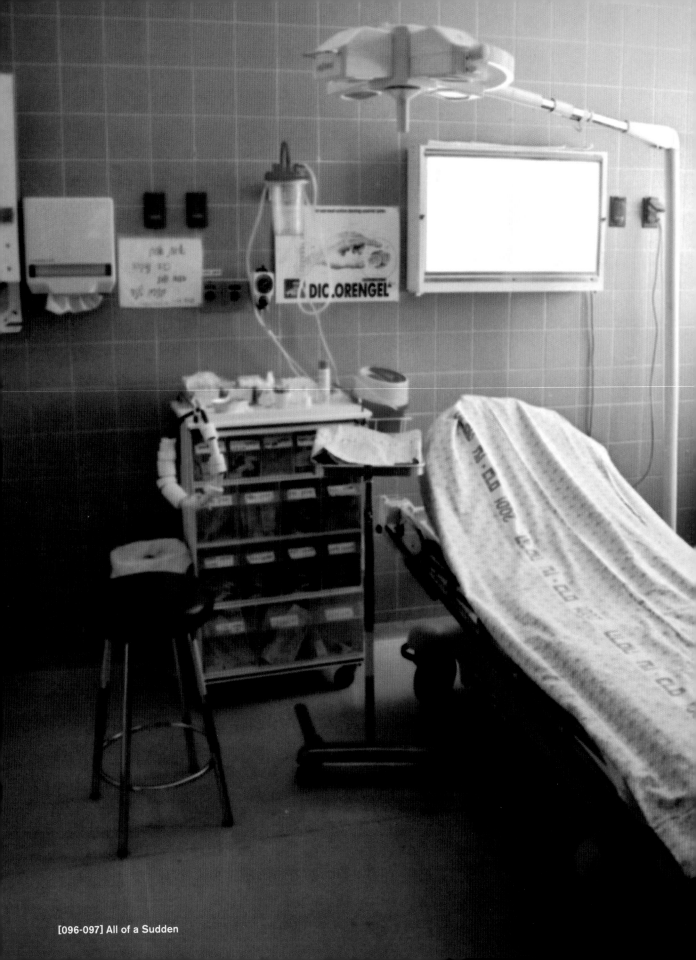

06 Identity

To be yourself; the fact that you are the one they are trying to get.

Identifying Details;

Given name:
Family name:
Age:
Date of attack:
Place of attack:
Place of residence:
Place of birth:
Date of birth:
Nationality:
Country of origin:
Sex:
Year of immigration:
Education:
Profession:
Military service:
Rank:
Color:
Next of kin:
(parents, brothers, sisters,
marital status, children):
Place of burial:
Hobbies:
Principles:
Achievements:
Loves:
Travel abroad:
Nickname:
Titles:
Positive characteristics:

Places of entertainment:	Style of dress:		
Friends:	Favorite food:		
Preferences:	Reserve duty:		
Characteristic remarks:	Areas of interest:		
Vision:	Favorite singer:		
Religion:	Book:	Height:	
Dreams:	Movie:	Weight:	
Political views:	Previous address:	Color of eyes:	
Ambitions:	Restaurant:	When last seen:	
Faith:	Character traits:	Last seen by whom:	Plans for the future:

מדרכי סבג (56) 27.2 מוצא הוא | קלוד קפאל (16) 1.3 צומת מרמל | מתי דין (85) 3.3 נתניה | סלומה מין (58) 3.3 נתניה | ובניה מלבין (71) 3.3 נתניה | בוגן כהן (59) 19.3 ירושלים | שלהבת פס (10) | מתן לבנקוב | אליזן רוזנברג (14) | דינה באהוב (48) 1.4 חיפה | הלבב קינן (23) 1.4 שבט

(מלואי שורות של תמונות זיכרון עם שמות, גילאים, תאריכים ומקומות — הטקסט בכתוביות קטנות מאוד ולא ניתן לקרוא את כולו בבירור)

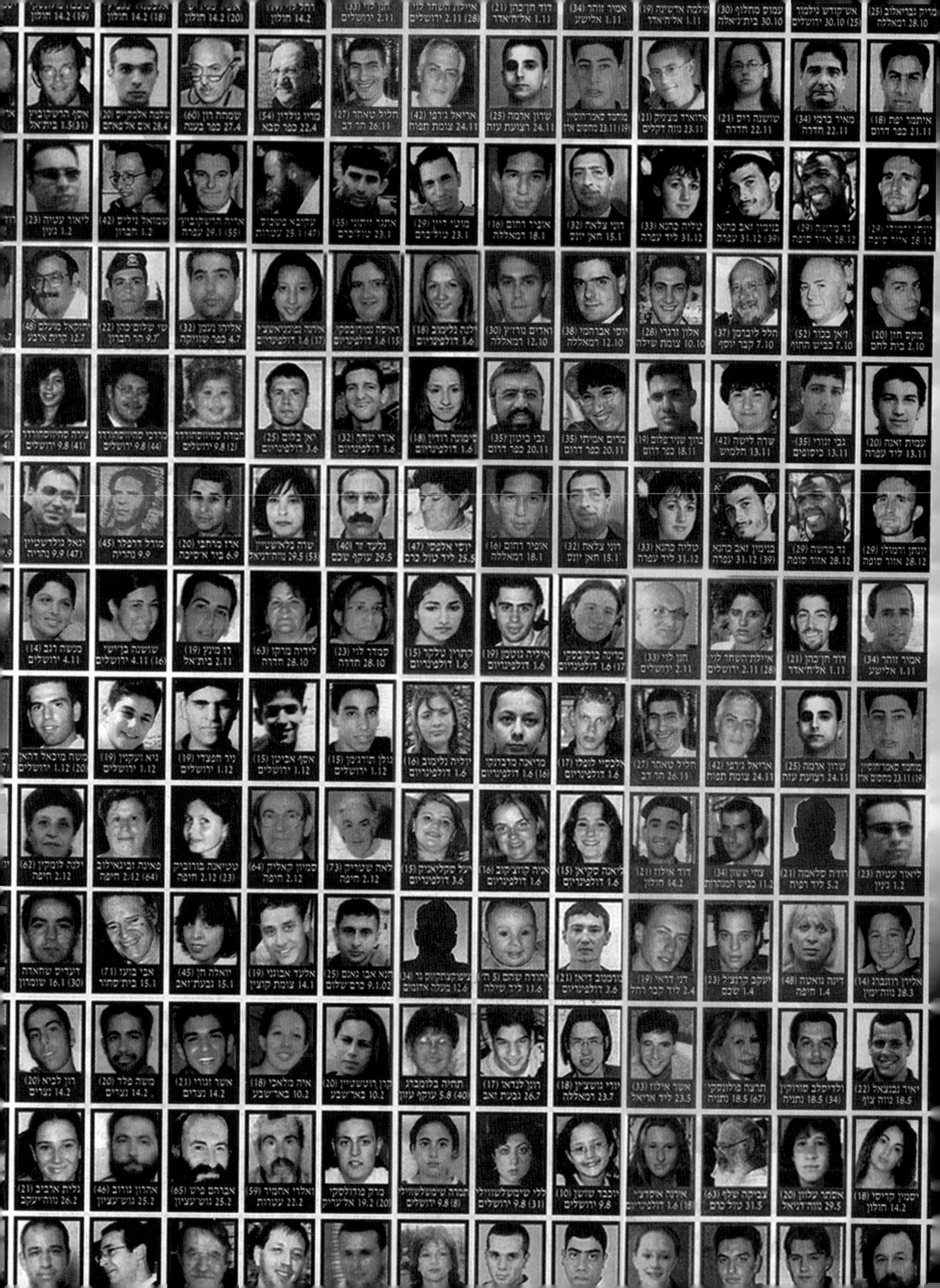

Look at the pictures of the next terrorist attack:

Blood, suffering, death are liable to be your fate tomorrow or in another week. A pointless, unnecessary death, without recompense or purpose. It can happen when you meet friends in a cafe, celebrate with family in a catering hall, walk innocently in the street or enjoy a typical night out in a nightclub. All of a sudden you'll hear a boom. All of a sudden you'll see a terrorist shooting in every direction. All of a sudden your entire life will change. You just happened to go to the cafe because it's near your house, you just happened to accept the invitation to the Bat Mitzva (because you couldn't get out of it), you just happened to be walking in the street (because you were coming home from work). For the most part you won't have any other, secret motive. Going out to enjoy yourself won't be a symbolic, declarative act. It won't be meant to convey any message. It won't be for any lofty purpose. You will just be having a good time, without any ideological overtones.

Your death will be meaningless. You will die for nothing. Your death will not contribute anything to the general welfare. You will not have sacrificed your life for an important goal. And you will not be remembered as one who did. The country won't owe you a thing.

To live without purpose is fine. To die without purpose, unnecessarily, arouses anger. It is intolerable. As a potential victim you should know that if you die in a terrorist attack no significance will attach to your presence at the site of the outrage. You are not a symbol and you don't represent anything, you are just an insignificant statistic in the march of folly. The tragedy of your death will derive its force specifically from its purposelessness and needlessness. Your puddle of blood on the sidewalk will have no value. You just happened to be there. You had a highly developed mechanism of repression. You said it will never happen to you. You ignored the statistics and the probabilities. You gambled. You hoped. As for everyone else, it didn't make sense to you that you would die. Not yet.

Because you're still young. Because it isn't fair. Because you had plans. Because you didn't want to die.

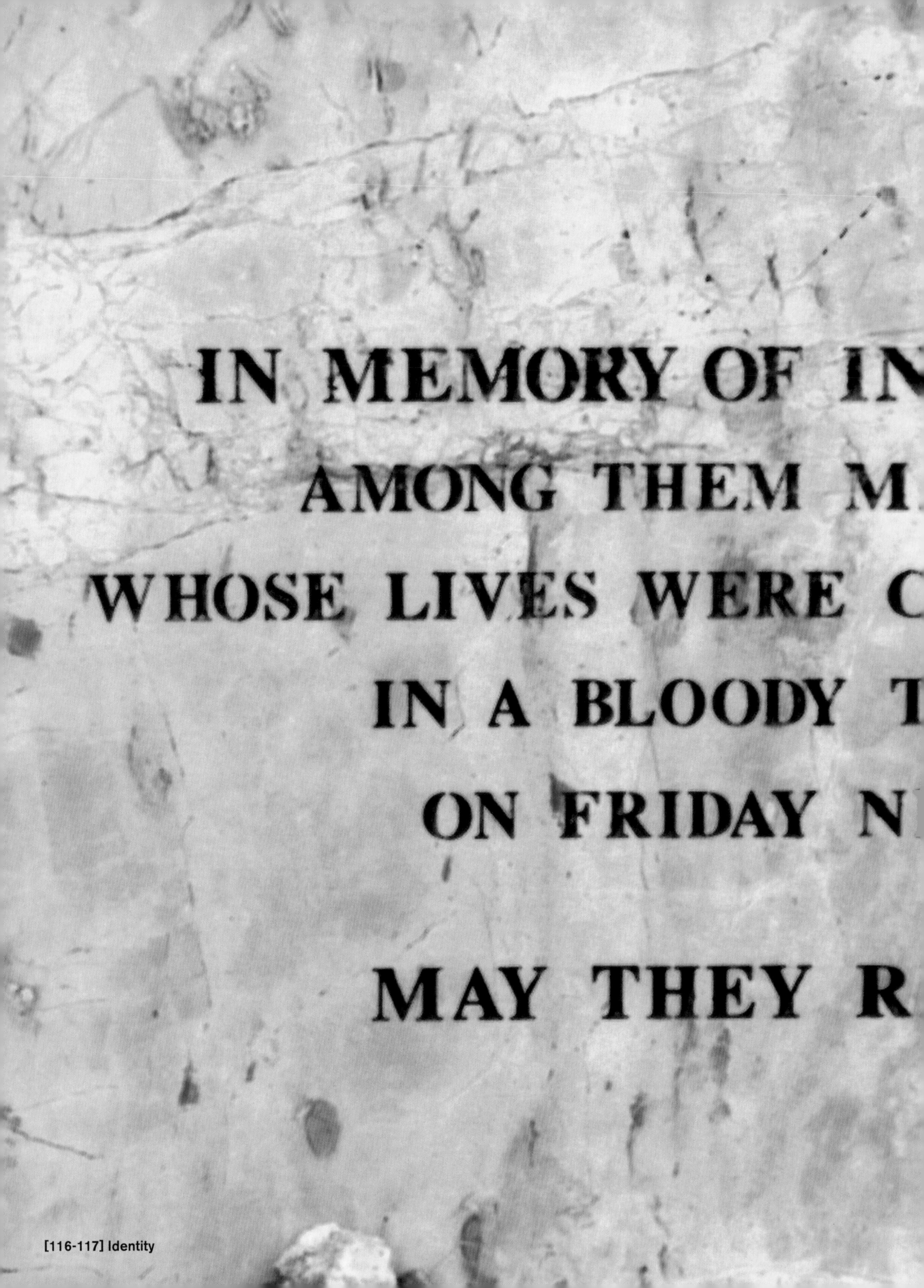

IN MEMORY OF IN

AMONG THEM M

WHOSE LIVES WERE C

IN A BLOODY T

ON FRIDAY N

MAY THEY R

OCENT CITIZENS

NY YOUNGSTERS

T OFF BY MURDERERS

RROR ATTACK

HT 1. 6. 2001

ST IN PEACE

State of Siege

07 Maybe

Maybe this time it's you

City Center

Jerusalem map

[122-123] maybe

Maybe this
Maybe this
Maybe this
Maybe this

[124-125] maybe

08 Survival

Watch Your Step: A Guide for Survival

DANGER

כניסה אסורה!

الدخول ممنوع !

FIRING AREA ENTRAN

סכנה

שטח אש ה.

خطر

منطقة اطلاق ال

E FORBIDDEN!

The Street

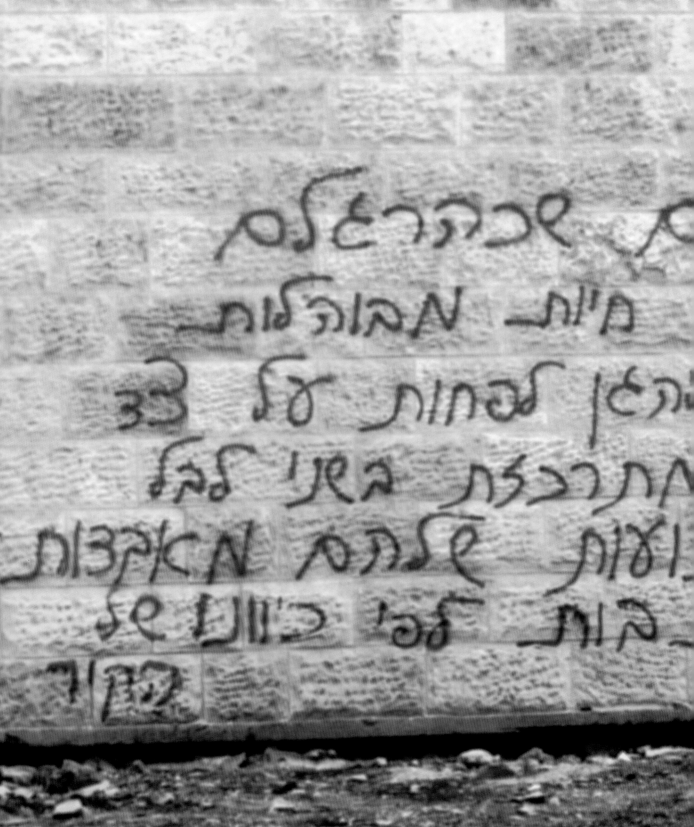

There are people who are in the habit of walking close to the wall, like frightened animals. They think they'll be

be hit from there. And in this way their movements lose their freedom and are dictated by the course of the wall.

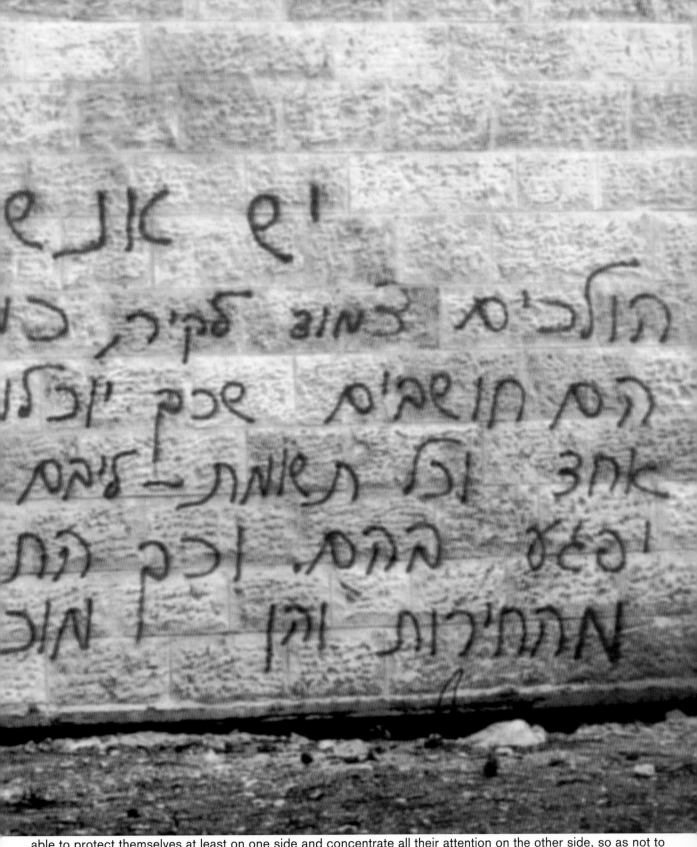

able to protect themselves at least on one side and concentrate all their attention on the other side, so as not to

Know that when you are walki

Especially in places full of people, in public places, in cafes, catering halls, markets, pedestrian malls and even crosswalks. bomber, car bomb, gunman, stabber or in any other hostile

in the street you are a target!

in shopping malls, on buses, in train stations, nightclubs,
In any place and at any time you are liable to be hit by a suicide
terrorist event.

Keep up normal life

1. Find alternative routes for driving and walking in the street.
2. Learn the location of the police stations, hospitals and army camps in your area.
3. Avoid loitering or parking in dark places as much as possible.
4. Try to walk close to the walls of buildings or concrete emplacements and sandbags so that you can take cover in time of need.
5. Avoid standing in line at the entrances of crowded places, especially near guards.
6. Don't go to any place that doesn't have a guard, and even then look around for suspicious persons.

A bullet proof wall in a Jerusalem neighborhood

7. When going to (obligatory) family gatherings, check out the security arrangements.

8. Don't go to cafes/restaurants/nightclubs unless you have to.

9. Go to small places on side streets with few people.

10. Don't sit near the entrance of a cafe or restaurant. Suicide bombers tend to blow themselves up there.

11. In open places, sit facing and close to the exit so that you can escape if the need arises.

12. Go to places that have already been attacked; they're considered safer.

13. Finish eating quickly and leave / order takeaway food.

Stay alert

14. Imagine possible attack scenarios and plan your responses accordingly.

15. Always look for suspicious objects, even in the most ordinary places and in every possible form.

16. Study passersby and try to spot suspicious signs, such as:

    a. a person [male or female] of Eastern-Arab appearance aged 20-50 with an attaché case or any other suspicious object/with an explosive belt around the pelvis resembling a paunch or pregnancy.

    b. signs of nervousness: sweat, restlessness, tension.

    c. a fearful look, a strange look or expressionless eyes.

17. If you encounter a terrorist, a suspicious person or a suspicious object, notify the police or any other security personnel in the area.

Dial [911]

The Bus

The bus is a high-quality target for the terrorist: the concentration of many people in a closed space, lends greater force to the explosion and causes a higher number of casualties. Furthermore, bus windows are transparent and thus make passengers easy targets for gunfire whether the bus is in motion or at a bus stop.

Bus stops and the buses themselves are public places that are seldom guarded, which enables the terrorist to get to them with relative ease.

פטיש בטחון!
לשבירת זכוכית בעת סכנה

SECURITY HAMMER
FOR BREAKING GLAS

شاكوش أمن لتحطيم الزجاج في
حالات الخطر

[↓]STOP! Have you forgotten something on the bus?　　　　　　　　　[↑]In case of danger, break glass

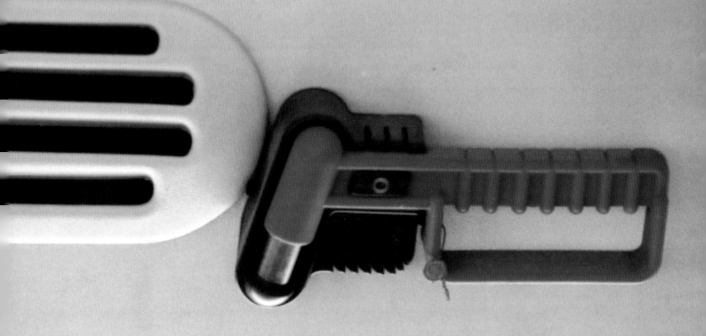

עמוד
השכחת משהו
בתור האוטובוס?

נוסע נכבד !

סרוק סביב מקום מושבך

ודווח לנהג על כל חפץ חשוד

זכור : ערנות מונעת אסון !!!

[↑]Dear Passenger! Check the area around your seat and report any suspicious object to the driver

פתח בטחון !

נפץ זגוגית במקרה סכנה

EMERGENCY EXIT!

افتح باب الرزع عند الخطر

ט' 2936

A bus stop

פתח בטחון!
נפץ זגוגית במקרה סכנה
EMERGENCY EXIT!
افتح باب الزجاج عند الخطر

בעת סכנה יש לדחוף
בעזרת הרגל את
החלון כולו -כלפי חוץ

Prayer for Travelers

1. Avoid riding on a bus; walking or traveling by car or taxi is preferable.

2. Don't wait for a bus at the bus stop, unless you're the first one there. Wait in a protected place or across the street.

3. Prepare your change or bus ticket beforehand so that you won't have to stand next to the driver too long.

4. If you're carrying any baggage, keep it close by, under lock and key, or in sight. If you place anything in the baggage compartment of the bus, make sure to mark it for easy identification. Before opening a bag that wasn't within sight, make sure no one touched it.

5. Don't sit at the front of the bus. A terrorist suspected by the driver blows himself up immediately.

6. Don't sit in the middle of the bus. Experience shows that a suicide bomber never goes past the middle of the bus, aiming to blow himself up there.

7. Take your place next to someone already seated, who doesn't look suspicious. In this way undesirable types won't be able to sit down next to you.

8. Try not to sit next to the window. In this way you'll be less exposed.

In the Event of an Attack

1. If you find yourself in the area of an attack, lie face down on the ground with your hands over your head the moment you hear a blast.

2. If you have not sustained medium to critical injuries, get up and distance yourself from the area, to avoid additional bombs. Try to help other injured.

3. In the event of a shooting incident, try to take cover: stairwells, concrete emplacements or any other bulletproof hiding place. If you are near the terrorist and unarmed, lie face down on the ground to minimize the chances of being hit.

4. If you are hit, wait for the rescue and security forces to evacuate you.

5. If you have identified an armed terrorist while standing in line or at a bus stop, shout: "Terrorist! Get down" and lie down on the ground. If you are armed, try to kill him. Avoid at all costs injuring innocent civilians.

6. If you are riding in a bus that is fired on from a passing car or a roadside ambush, lie down on the floor and protect your head with your hands.

7. If there is an explosion on the bus, get out in case of additional bombs or gunfire. Try to escape via the doors or windows (use the emergency hammer).

8. If you have identified a suspicious vehicle moving near the bus, report it to the driver.

9. In case of any incident, call the police [911].

BULLET
PROOF
VEST
FOR
5.56   7.62
9 mm
800$
 וסט קראמי
נגד כדורים
קלאצניקוב
16-m
9MM

The Survival Kit

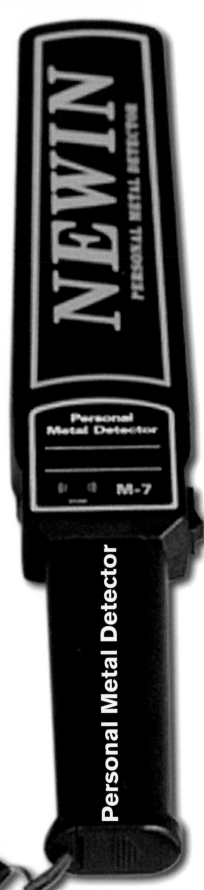

Personal Metal Detector

Transistor Radio

Enables you to keep informed about incidents, attacks, responses and - above all - warnings.

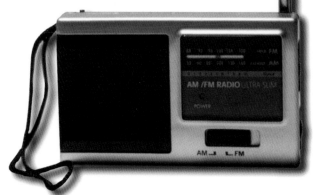

Cellular Phone

Blood Donation

Donate your blood to a Magen David Adom blood bank. In this way you'll be insured and may even save a life.

Know Your Blood Type

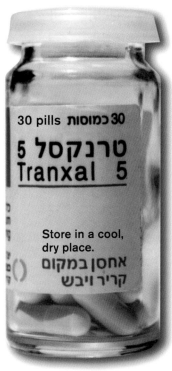

Tranquilizers

Pressure and tension make it necessary to take pills against anxiety and depression.

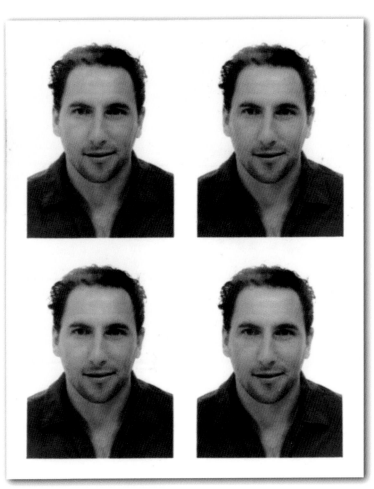

Gas Mask

It is recommended to keep a gas mask in the baggage compartment of your car.

Murder Photo

Prepare in advance a high-quality passport photo in case your picture needs to appear in the newspapers.

First Aid Kit

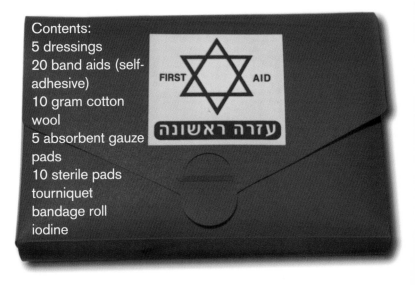

Contents:
5 dressings
20 band aids (self-adhesive)
10 gram cotton wool
5 absorbent gauze pads
10 sterile pads
tourniquet
bandage roll
iodine

A mall in Jerusalem

Is there anything that can still shock you?

Israeli policeman taking control after a terror attack

That ca

you unc

make

erstand

Where you're living

That it can't go
on like this

09 Action
Dealing with the situation

A big ch

The ordinary Israeli has become s

The funerals of terror victims have become m

occurr

restrained, closed, bewildered, gloor

When Israel began liquidating those who send the terrorists, Israelis were aroused somewh

typica

attacks did this, and the feeling of h

the Israelis put their feelings on the back burner. The sense of helplessness during the mounti

arroga

and they becam

happening. Few still had the hope a

hothead

ange has

nber, introverted, serious, taciturn,

nd more quiet, many of them conducted quickly.

d in the

complicated and very unfriendly. The

ough not like before the wave of attacks. It would seem that during the months of restraint,

brash,

lessness closed them up completely

tacks, even after the big military actions, changed to apathy and lack of interest in what was

t, loud,

nured to feeling.

ith that they would see better days.

ed Israeli.

["] Orli Castel - Blum, Human Parts

The Silent Majority

Most Israelis sat at home in front of their television sets, sighed and shook their heads in despair.
Nevertheless, a few took to the streets and voiced their protest, despite the situation and because of it.

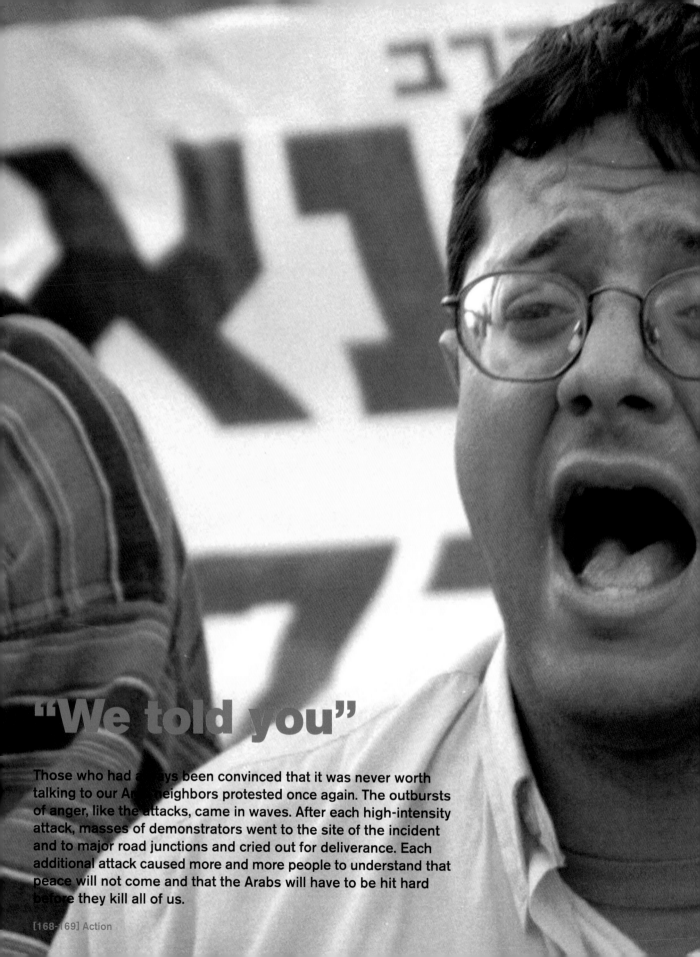

"We told you"

Those who had always been convinced that it was never worth talking to our Arab neighbors protested once again. The outbursts of anger, like the attacks, came in waves. After each high-intensity attack, masses of demonstrators went to the site of the incident and to major road junctions and cried out for deliverance. Each additional attack caused more and more people to understand that peace will not come and that the Arabs will have to be hit hard before they kill all of us.

Rescind the
Palestinian
Charter

Peres Is a
War
Criminal

The Time Has
Come to Live

Bring the
Oslo Criminals to
Justice

No
Expulsion
for Jews

Vengeanc

Arabs Out

Kahane Was
Right

No Arabs, No Attacks	**Hats Off to the IDF**
Don't Give Them a State / **Israel Will Be Liberated in Blood**	**A Good Arab Is a Dead Arab**
Throw Out the Arabs	**Bibi or Ahmed Tibi** **Long Live the People of Israel**
Death to the Arabs	**The Left Is a Cancer in the Heart of the Nation**

Opposed to them, at the extreme left of the political spectrum,
business went on as usual, with the mantra:

Every Friday, between the hours of 10 a.m. and 3 p.m. women dressed in black
stood in the less central road junctions. Usually alone, they waved signs calling
for an end to the occupation. Their outlook, which, before the state of siege, had
been more accepted, were now a minority view and they were subjected to harsh
criticism and insults from passersby, but they continued their protest.

צבא ביבוש
צבא טהור
הפשיעם לא
יעבור

תסתכלו במראה
תראו את היטלר

Summer of Love
WiZdom
Winter please

התנחלות!

Help

All Armies of
Occupation Are Armies
of Terror
The Crimes Will Not Be
Forgotten

Racism   Wars
No ~~Arabs~~ No ~~Attacks~~

Look in the Mirror
You Can See Hitler

Zionism = Racism

There's a Border
There's a Rectification

Occupation =
Terrorism

It's Good to Die for
One's Settlement?

All People Were Created in the Image of God	**No Peace without Evacuating the Settlements**
4-F No Shooting and No Tears	**Long Live the Underground Death to Zionism** **No to War Between Nations No to Peace Between Stratas**
Resist	**Down with the Occupation**
Sharon, You Promised Peace, You Brought Another War	

Destroy the Palestinian Authority

The Land of Israel
for the People of Israel
No Arabs = No Attacks
Let the IDF Fight
Transfer Now
Kahane Was Right
Death
To the Arabs

End the Occupation

And there were those who sought a different way:

Escapism

Soap operas broke the rating records,
travel abroad continued, fashion, cooking magazines and talk
shows were popular, a few began to think about emigration.

Our Father Who Art in Heaven

There were those who out of despair and lack of faith in the nation's leaders understood that they had no one to rely on other than the Almighty.

Blue and White

In the absence of a real solution to the situation, nothing was left to the leaders of the nation but to strengthen the people by calling on them to rally around the flag and find consolation in what remained of Israeli pride.

[↓] We Wave the Flag. We Shall Continue to Live the Dream   [↑] I'm a Patriot - Sonol gas company advertisement

[↑] Israel Buys Blue and White advertisement Ministry of Commerce   [↓] This Country Cannot Be Stopped

Volunteer to Prevent the Next Attack!
Contact the Civil Guard base nearest to your home]

["] Posted on billboards throughout the country by Civil Guard volunteers.

10 Continuity

"I know and you know that you're not allowed to touch a suspicious object, or go near it." A part of educational television message for Israeli children

Childhood

Palestinian teenagers stoning Israeli soldiers

alestinian infant wearing explosives

What Do Y
To Be If Yo

ou Want
Grow Up?

11 Faith and Power

Story of the power of faith and the faith in power

Faith and power

and different faiths

Two peoples living together

without borders

with the same dream

A struggle arose

Palestinian youth rioting

A Palestinian flags his bloody hands to the roaring crowd after lynching two Israelis in Ramallah

At times, through the power of faith, one loses one's humanity

and at times, through faith in power, one loses one's reason

שלום

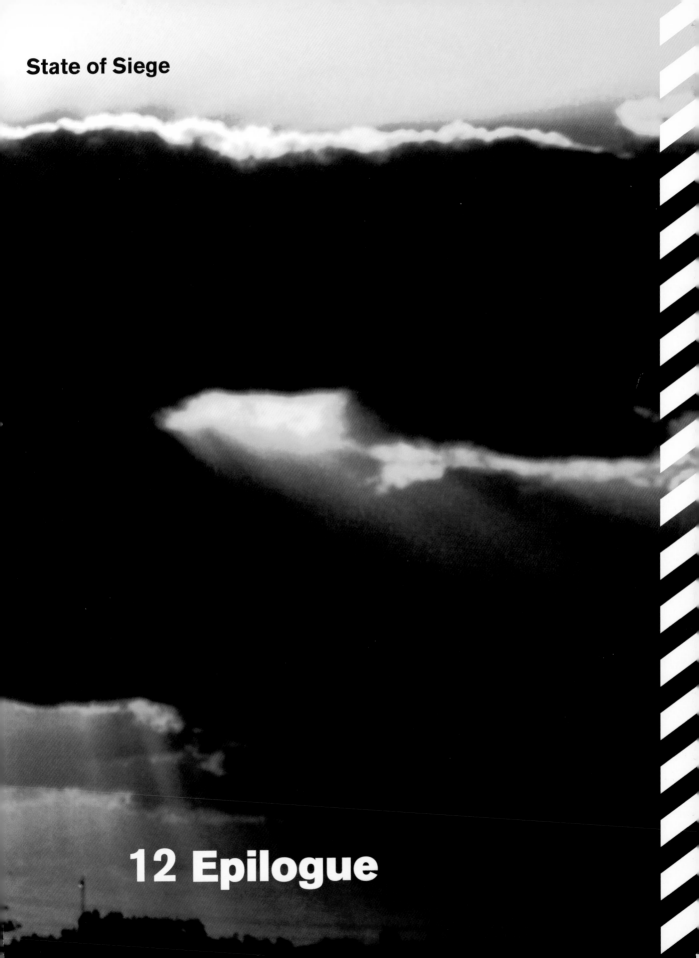

State of Siege

12 Epilogue

וְכִתְּתוּ חַרְבֹתֵיהֶם לְאִתִּים

גוֹי אֶל־גּוֹי חֶרֶב וְלֹא־יִלְמְדוּן

גֶּפְנוֹ וְתַחַת תְּאֵנָתוֹ וְאֵין

(מיכה ד, פסוק ג-ד)

And they shall beat their swords
into pruning hooks: nation shall
neither shall they learn war any
under his vine and under his fi
afraid . . .

וַחֲנִיתֹתֵיהֶם לְמַזְמֵרוֹת לֹא־יִשָּׂ

עוֹד מִלְחָמָה: וְיָשְׁבוּ אִישׁ

מַחֲרִיד

...to plowshares, and their spears

...ot lift up a sword against nation,

...ore. But they shall sit every man

...ree: and none shall make them

[MICHA 4, 3-4]

List of photographs, illustrations and credits

[Photographs not credited to a photographer were taken by the Author]

[003] Sand bags - Gilo, Jerusalem, April 2002. [004-005] Open graves - Givat Shaul, Jerusalem, April 2002. [006-007] Bottles for recycling - Tel Aviv, April 2002. [008-009] "Statue of Liberty" -Talpiot Industrial area, Jerusalem, 2002. [010] Paratroopers - from the book "1,000 days," 1967. [012-013] 1968 - Filling sand bags. 1969 - Tending to the injured at the Suez Canal. 1970 - Terrorist attack in Avivim - Moshe Milner, G.P.O. 1971 - Artillery on Beit Shean - Ya'acov Sa'ar - G.P.O. 1973 - Evacuating casualties during the Yom Kippur War - David Rubingar - G.P.O. 1974 - Terror attack in Ma'alot - Israel Simionski - G.P.O. 1978 - Terror attack, the coastal road near Tel Aviv - Shmuel Rachmany - G.P.O. 1982 - Lebanon War - Yoel Kantor - G.P.O. 1985 - A terrorist killed in Southern Lebanon - Nabil Ismail, AFP. 1987 - The first Intifada - Thomas Coex, AFP. 1989 - Stabbing a reserve soldier - Awad Awad, AFP. 1991 - The Gulf War - Tsvika Israeli - G.P.O. 1993 - Beginning of the Oslo Accords - Awad Awad, AFP. 1994 - Terror attack in Tel Aviv - Ziv Koren. 1996 - Terror attack in Dizengoff St. - Ziv Koren. 1997 - Terror attack, Cafe Apropo, Tel Aviv - Michael Kramer . 1998 - The Kotel tunnel - Awad Awad, AFP. 1999 - In the "territories" - Thomas Coex, AFP. [014-015] Entry forbidden [00] - Gush Katif, Gaza Strip - Fayez Nureldine, AFP. [020] Policeman - Florentine, Tel Aviv, May 2002. [024] Flag - Hadera, May 2002. [032-033] King George, Jaffa St-Strauss intersection, Jerusalem - Duby Tal, Moni Haramati, Albatross from Kav Haofek, Jerusalem. [034-035] Aerial photo. [038] Terror attack in Ein Arich - Yediot Achronot - Guy Drucker. [039-040] Elimination of a terrorist in Nablus - Yediot Achronot - Itai R. [041-042] Bombing a Tank in Netzarim - Yediot Achronot - Itai R. [043] The falling of the Duvdevan unit in a combat accident - Ninio, published by "Ha'aretz", 17.02.2002 (c) "Ha'aretz" Daily Newspaper Ltd*. [044] Shooting at soldiers [2 illustrations] - Yediot Achronot - Guy Drucker. The accidental killing of a Givati officer - Ori Tzor, published by "Ha'aretz", 07.03.2002 (c) "Ha'aretz" Daily Newspaper Ltd*. The Car Bomb - Olga Zletkin, published by "Ha'aretz", 06.06.2002 (c) "Ha'aretz" Daily Newspaper Ltd*. The ambush in Jenin - Olga Zletkin, published by "Ha'aretz", 10.04.2002 (c) "Ha'aretz" Daily Newspaper Ltd*. Bombing a Tank in Netzarim 2 - Yediot Achronot - Itai R. [045] Terror attack in Rishon LeZion [2 illustrations] - Olga Zletkin, published by "Ha'aretz", 09.05.2002 (c) "Ha'aretz" Daily Newspaper Ltd*. Terror attack in Adura - Olga Zletkin, published by "Ha'aretz", 28.04.2002 (c) "Ha'aretz" Daily Newspaper Ltd*. Terror attack in Carmei Tzur [6 illustrations] - Olga Zletkin, published by "Ha'aretz", 09.06.2002 (c) "Ha'aretz" Daily Newspaper Ltd*. Attempted terror attack at Glilot oil depot - Yediot Achronot - Guy Drucker. [046-047] The massacre in Park Hotel - anonymous, published by "Ha'aretz", 29.03.2002 (c) "Ha'aretz" Daily Newspaper Ltd*. [048-049] Arafat's headquarters under siege in Ramallah - Yediot Achronot - Toby Ben Herzl. [054-055] Rabin murder - Graffiti in Florentine neighborhood, Tel Aviv. [056] Shimon Peres - 1992 - Michah Kirshner. [057] Bibi Netanyahu - Steak-house, Tel Aviv, April 2002. [058] Ehud Barak - Netivot-Be'er Sheba road, March 2002. [059] Ariel Sharon - Machane Yehuda market, Jerusalem, April 2002. [060-061] Yasser Arafat - Gaza Strip, 1994 - Manoocher Daghati, AFP. [062-063] Prime Minister's chambers - Jerusalem - Daniel Cohen. [066-079] Stills from TV broadcast. [080] Trauma room - Hadassah Ein Karem hospital, Jerusalem, May 2002. [088-089] A "high-casualty" drill of the

Hadassah Ein Karem hospital, Teddy Stadium, Jerusalem, May 2002. [092-093] Terror attack in Sbarro restaurant - King George St, Jerusalem - Daniel Cohen. [094-095] Terror attack on Jaffa St - Jerusalem - Daniel Cohen. [096] A bed in the emergency room - Hadassah Ein Karem, Jerusalem, May 1995. [097] X-Ray. [102-103] Routine - Khalil Dehaini, AFP. [104] Mail boxes - Har Chotzvim, Jerusalem, May 2002. [108-113] Photos of terror attacks' victims - Yediot Achronot. [116-117] Monument in memory of terror victims - Dolphinarium, Tel Aviv, June 2002. [122-123] Map of Central Jerusalem - Mapa. [124-125] People in Tel Aviv streets - May 2002. [126-127] Map of Manhattan. [128-129] Sand bags - Gilo, Jerusalem, April 2002. [130-131] Firing zone, Zeelim, March 2002. [132-133] A street in Hebron - September 1995 - Menahem Kahana, AFP. [134-135] Graffiti - Independence Park, Jerusalem, May 2002. [136-137] People - Beit Hadar, Talpiot, Jerusalem, May 2002. [138-139] A wall for protection in Gilo neighborhood - Jerusalem, April 2002. [140-141] Student's day at the Israel Museum - Jerusalem, May 2002. [142-143] A bus on Jaffa St - Jerusalem, April 2002. [144-145, 148-149] Stickers in a bus - Central Bus Station, Jerusalem, May 2002. [146-147] A bulletproof bus stop in Gilo - Jerusalem, April 2002. [150-151] Store window - Ben Yehuda St, Jerusalem. [152-153] Emergency Kit - Studio photography. [154] Search of suspicious objects - Malcha Mall, Jerusalem, March 2002 - Daniel Cohen. [156-157] Terror attack - Jaffa St, Jerusalem, 1998 - Yoav Lemmer - AFP. [158-159] Terror attack in pixels. [160] Terror attack at the Park Hotel - Netanya, Passover, April 2002 - Daniel Cohen. [161 above] Terror attack at the Sbarro restaurant - Jerusalem - Daniel Cohen. [161 bottom] Terror attack - Park Hotel, Netanya - Daniel Cohen. [166-167] Pinuk ad - Rabin Square, Tel Aviv, May 2002. [168-169] Protest of a right-wing activist - Daniel Cohen. [170-171] Nationalistic graffiti - at locations throughout the country. [174-175, 177] Flags - Zion Square, Jerusalem, May 2002. [176] Woman in black - Gan Shmuel, April 2002. [178-179] Leftist graffiti - at locations throughout the country. [184-185] The sky above the Negev, March 2002. [186] Baba Sali - Netivot, May 2002 - Ran Mendelson. [187] Burning candles - tomb of the Baba Sali, Netivot, May 2002. [187 bottom] King Messiah - Afula, April 2002. [188-189] Patriotic signs - at locations throughout the country. [190] Sign - civil guard in Kfar Tavor, April 2002. [192-193] Dolls - Machane Yehuda market, Jerusalem, May 2002. [194] Children - Kibbutz Na'an, January 2002. [195] "Toys" - Studio photography. [196 above] Plastic soldiers - Studio photography.[196 bottom] Palestinian teenagers stoning Israeli soldiers - Anonymous. [197] A Palestinian infant wearing explosives - Anonymous. [198-199] "Toys" - Studio photography. [202] Prayer - Beth Lechem, October 1996 - Menahem Kahana, AFP. [203] Temple Mount - Jerusalem, August 2000. [204-205] "Rendez-vous" of Israelis and Palestinians - Jenin - Pavel Walenberg. [206-207] Field - Kfar Tavor, March 2002. [208-209] Confrontation - Ramallah, September 2000 - Daniel Cohen. [210] Confrontation, Hebron, March 1997, Thomas Koex, AFP. [211] Burning tire - Ramallah, May 2002. [212-213] Lynching of Israeli soldiers - Ramallah, October 2000 - Chris Gerald, AFP. [214-215] Ruins - Jenin, April 2002 - Sagi Blumberg. [216-217] Sunset - Lod, May 1999. [220] Girl with Israeli flag, Ben Yehuda St, Jerusalem, May 2002. [221] Candle.

This book was produced as a graduation project
in the Department of Visual Communications
Bezalel Academy of Art and Design, Jerusalem

This book would have never been published without
 the tremendous help of:
Joey Low, Adi Stern, Shimon Zandhouse,
Daniel Cohen, Elad Mishan, Sagi Blumberg,
Ran Mendelson, Geva, Dov Avramson,
Amit Shaham.

Also thanks to Ilan Greenfield and Irit Alhassid
from Gefen Publishing House.

And my gratitude to those dearest to me,
my loving and supportive family: Mom, Dad, Nadav,
Yoval, and Reut. My grandparents Rivka and David,
and the one that was everything, Maya Mor.

This book was produced out of love
for the State of Israel with hope for better days.